GREAT GRANDMA'S RECIPES

GREAT GRANDMA'S RECIPES

Victoria Oladuti Adegoroye

PYXIDIA HOUSE PUBLISHERS

GREAT GRANDMA'S RECIPES
Copyright©2023 by Victoria Oladuti Adegoroye.

Request for information on this title should be addressed to
Victoria Oladuti Adegoroye
Email: tapsbp@gmail.com, soladb2010@gmail.com, temil88@yahoo.com, willowforest@outlook.com

Library of Congress Cataloging-in-Publication Data

Victoria Oladuti Adegoroye
GREAT GRANDMA'S RECIPES
ISBN-13: 978-1-946530-41-7 (Paperback)
ISBN-10: 1-946530-41-7 (Paperback)
1. Cooking - Recipes - Non-fiction 1. Title
Library of Congress Control Number: 2023933585

Edited by Winnie Aduayi
Designed by Rick Simmons

Published in Dallas Texas by Pyxidia House Publishers.
A registered trademark of Pyxidia Concept llc.
www.pyxidiahouse.com
info@pyxidiahouse.com

Printed in the United States of America

To My LORD and SAVIOUR, JESUS CHRIST, who has preserved me over the years and blessed me beyond measure.

Psalm 18:2
The LORD is my rock, and my fortress, and my deliverer; my GOD, my strength, in whom I will trust; my buckler, and the horn of my salvation, and my high tower.

Acknowledgements

I would like to thank my children, who came up with the idea for this cookbook. My grandchildren supported the idea and took this forward, with my granddaughter Temilade acting as the scribe.

Thank you Tolu, Sola, Sade, Tinuade, Temilade and Kemi for contributing your recipes to enrich this cookbook.

I am thankful that my love for cooking and baking has been passed down to my granddaughters, Temitayo and Onose, and my great-granddaughter, Areli.

Above all, I am grateful to The LORD for HIS Grace over my life and for giving me this talent.

Contents

Family Specialties With Great Grandma

Introduction

Nigeria is a cradle of lavish feasting, epitomized in its special delicacies. For thousands of years, food and hospitality have been thickly woven into a culture bursting with tradition, and at its axis is the family and community. There remains a myth that Nigerian cooking is cumbersome and time-consuming – this book offers guidance on how Nigerian cooking can be made simple, based on these classic recipes of Great Grandma.

As the matriarch of the family, I have spent over 70 years preparing delicious meals for three generations – my children, grandchildren, and great grandchildren. My meals bring back fond memories of family gatherings, and the very smell of Great Grandma's sumptuous cake leaves you nostalgic for the festive season. Many have often complimented my meals on being enjoyable, and rightfully so, as these meals get your taste buds singing for joy.

The nucleus of the culinary repertoire of *Great Grandma's Recipes* is the home kitchen, and in there, one can quite easily see that my cooking is an expression of my love for God and others, which my faith exemplifies. These recipes are a labor of love that captures my journey with food from my early years growing up in the rustic town of Akure and, subsequently, the bustling city of Lagos, both in Nigeria, West Africa, to my educational ventures in the United Kingdom and subsequent exposure to various cultures and flavours. This food journey continued during my marriage, where I lived with my husband, in different countries in Europe and Africa, with frequent trips to the United States of America.

With the growing and expanding family, I was inspired to leave this legacy of recipes for my offspring, posterity, and the world. My experiences and memories set the tone for what great cooking means to my family and inspired this body of work, *Great Grandma's Recipes.*

Great Grandma's Recipes is designed for everyday quick meals and special celebrations. The anatomy of an everyday home-style Nigerian meal weaves around a principal dish, such as stews, rice, and soups; this tends to remain true even for special celebrations. The recipes here will inspire you to make this cookbook an important part of your active culinary collection.

All the recipes in this cookbook are made with real, nourishing ingredients; you won't find any processed foods here. The cooking style here uses traditional foods – the food that our great-great-grandmothers cooked. This means *Great Grandma's Recipes* cooking is done with whole foods and uses practices that promote healthy nutrition and digestion. However, feel free to tailor these recipes to your own dietary needs.

Summarily, this is inviting you to a home-cooked meal on great grandma's table, which also includes a recipe tale on cooking the Nigerian way. I hope *Great Grandma's Recipes* helps take the stress out of cooking and gives you back real, from scratch, delicious home cooking for your family and guests.

Main Dishes

Whether you're celebrating the day's success or craving comfort
from life's storms, a warm richly-flavored meal at the end
of each day can can greatly appease the senses.

Tasty Pepper Stew

INGREDIENTS (Serves 7)

- 2 Big Red Pointed Sweet Peppers
- 1 Large Red Sweet Pepper
- 2 Scotch Bonnet Peppers
- 3/4 of an Onion
- 4 Tomatoes
- Tomato Puree (50g)
- 2 Cooking Spoons of Sunflower Oil
- 2 Chicken Knorr Cubes (900ml stock)
- 1 Beef Knorr Stock Pot 28g (Or Beef Stock)
- 7 Chicken Pieces, or 7 Lamb Pieces,
or 7 Beef Pieces.
- Seasoning (*1 Teaspoon of black pepper,
1 teaspoon of white pepper, 1 teaspoon of thyme,
1/2 teaspoon of salt*).

METHOD

Step 1
Wash the Chicken, Lamb or Beef, then sprinkle seasoning. Boil or bake for 20 minutes (*Flip it over on the other side after 10 minutes*).

Blend the peppers, onion, and toma... ntil smooth.

Step 2
Heat the sunflower oil in a cooking pot.

Step 3
Pour the Blended ingredients into the hot oil.

Step 4
Cover and cook on Medium heat for 15 minutes.

Step 5
Add the tomato puree, then stir and cook for 3 minutes.

Step 6
Add the knorr cubes, then stir and cook for 5 minutes.

Step 7
Add the chicken, lamb, or beef (or a combination of two or all) and leave for 15 minutes on medium heat.

Vegetable Soup

INGREDIENTS (Serves 2)

- 3 Bundles of Green Vegetables (*Tete or Soko*)
- Dry Fish
- 6 – 10 *Ata Rodo* (Scotch Bonnet Peppers)
- 4 Onions
- 5 Tablespoons of Groundnut Oil
- Water

METHOD

Step 1

Cut and wash vegetables thoroughly. Boil enough water, pour in the vegetables and cover for 10 minutes. Vegetables should be green by quickly rinsing them in cold water.

Step 2

Pour groundnut oil into the cooking pot and let it fry. Include chopped onions until sizzling, then add the chopped *Ata Rodo* (scotch bonnet pepper) and fry well.

Step 3

Add dry fish and cook well, then add salt to taste. Cover it to cook on medium heat. After 10 minutes, stir well.

Step 4

When the soup is well cooked, add vegetables and stir — Cover and cook for 5 minutes. Uncover and put the vegetable soup in a serving bowl.

Your vegetable soup should remain green and ready to serve.

Okro Asepo

INGREDIENTS (Serves 2)

- Okro
- 5 Tablespoons of Crayfish
- 5 *Ata Rodo* (Scotch Bonnet Peppers)
- *Kaun* (Potash)
- 3 Tablespoons of Groundnut Oil
- Seasoning and Salt

METHOD

Step 1
Wash the okro and clean it in cold water. Cut the okro into very small pieces.

Step 2
Add water to the pot and add *Kaun* (potash). Put the cut okro in the pot to simmer and allow it to draw.

Step 3
Add pepper, crayfish, seasoning, and salt to taste. Lastly, add oil.

Step 4
Keep stirring quickly on a high flame for a short term to maintain the drawing. Remove from the fire and place in a cool place. *Do not cover when still hot.

Ewedu Soup

INGREDIENTS (Serves 2)

- *Ewedu* (Jute Leaves)
- 2 Tablespoons of Locust Beans
- 1/4 Tablespoon of *Kaun* (Potash)

METHOD 1

Step 1
Cut ewedu from stick and wash in cold water.

Step 2
Add water to the pot and add kaun. Include ewedu when water starts boiling.

Step 3
Start beating it with a local *Ijabe* (traditional broom) until *Ewedu* is soft, smooth, and drawing.

METHOD 2

Another method of preparing *Ewedu* is to liquidize it with water. Put it in a pot, add *kaun* (potash), boil it and keep stirring until it draws. Quickly add the locust beans while stirring on hot heat for one minute.

Do not overcook, so it doesn't lose its drawing. Do not cover until cold.

Serve with *Gbegiri*, stew, and *amala*.

Apon Soup

INGREDIENTS (Serves 2)

- 1 Large Tin of *Apon* (Seed of African Mango)
- 1 Spoon of *Iru* (fermented and processed locust beans)
- ½ Tablespoon of Dry Pepper
- Dry Fish & Dry Shrimps
- Pieces of Meat
- 1/4 Onion
- Salt

METHOD

Step 1
Remove the skin of the apon and grind the apon with some palm oil.

Step 2
Wash the meat and put it in a cooking pot. Add salt, seasoning and onions.

Step 3
Cook meat until soft. Add *iru* (fermented and processed locust beans), pepper, and onions.

Jollof Rice

INGREDIENTS (Serves 10)

- 2 Fresh Tomatoes
- 15 Fresh Peppers
- 2 Sachets of Tomato Paste
- 5 *Tatashe* (Red Bell Peppers)
- 2 Whole Onions
- 1 Ginger
- 4 Cloves of Garlic
- 3 Carrots
- 4 Cups of Rice
- Spices (Bay leaf, Curry, Thyme, Jollof rice spice)
- 1 Cup of Chicken or Beef stock
- Seasoning Cubes

METHOD

Step 1
Parboil 4 cups of rice and set aside.

Step 2
Blend the pepper mixture (tomato, *tatashe* [red bell pepper], *shombo* (cayenne pepper), garlic, ginger, onions) and boil.

Step 3
Chop onions and carrot.

Step 4
Heat the pot and add groundnut oil until hot.

Step 5
Pour chopped onions into the hot oil and add 2 sachets of tomato paste – fry for 5 minutes.

Step 6
Once the pepper mixture comes to a boil, add to the hot oil. Fry the mixture for another 5 minutes.

Step 7
Add 1 cup of stock, spices, and 3 seasoning cubes.

Step 8
Cover the pot to cook for 5 minutes, then add the chopped carrot to the pan.

Step 9
Finally, add the washed rice and allow it to cook until soft.

Fried Rice

INGREDIENTS (Serves 10)

- 4 cups of Rice
- Vegetables (Carrot, green pepper, spring onions, sweet corn)
- Groundnut oil
- Fresh pepper
- Onions
- Curry
- 1 Ginger
- 4 gloves of garlic
- Fried rice spice
- Shrimps
- Seasoning cubes

METHOD

Step 1
Boil four cups of rice and set aside.

Step 2
Heat the pan and add some groundnut oil.

Step 3
When hot, add onions, garlic, and ginger, then fry until sizzling.

Step 4
Add shrimps or chicken and stir fry for 5 minutes.

Step 5
Add your chopped vegetables to the mix.

Step 6
Include spices, a pinch of salt and 3 seasoning cubes.

Step 7
Finally, add the boiled rice and allow it to cook on low heat.

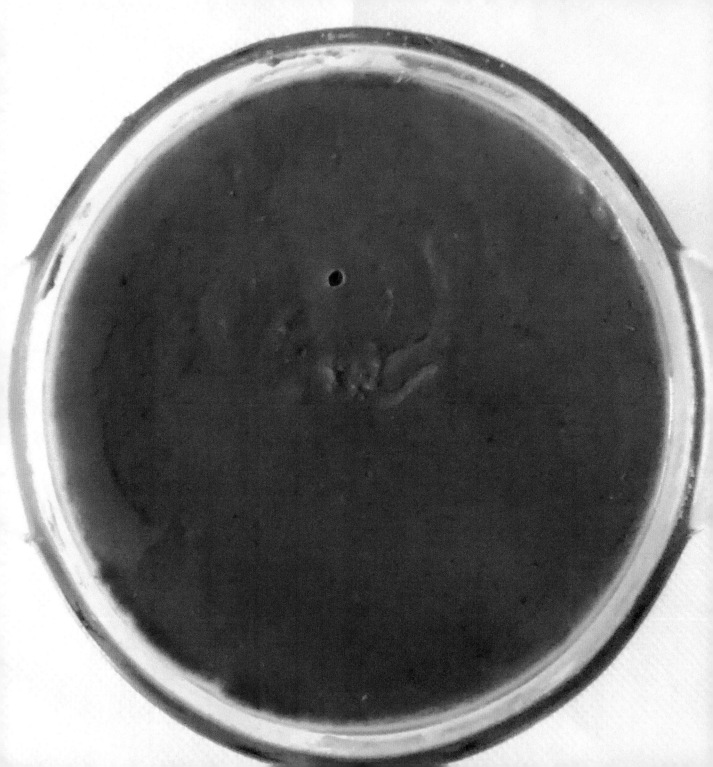

Frejon

INGREDIENTS (Serves 8)

- 1 kg Brown Beans
- 750mls Coconut Milk
- Sugar
- Bay Leaves Spices
- 1 Tablespoon of Cinnamon
- 7 Tablespoons of Honey
- 2 Tablespoons of Garlic

METHOD

Step 1
Boil beans with water until half cooked.
Add bay leaves, and cloves until well cooked and soft.

Step 2
Add coconut milk when the beans is almost cooked, and sugar for taste. Add cinnamon and cook until very soft. When properly cooked, you will blend it very smoothly to your taste and texture.

Step 3
Serve hot with fish stew.

Cakes

With its sweet glaze, cakes are quite the perfect accompaniment
to food and drinks. Rich and moist with a hearty and solid
flavour, it's quite the popular choice with many who
love to sweetly tease the tastebuds.

Sponge Cake

INGREDIENTS

- Butter – 1kg
- Sugar – 750g
- Softener – 2-Teaspoon
- Vanilla Essence – 2 Teaspoons
- Egg – 15 Large Eggs
- Flour – 1kg
- Baking Powder – 2 Tablespoons

METHOD

Step 1
Add the butter and sugar, then mix.
While mixing, add your softener and vanilla essence and mix very well.

Step 2
Beat your eggs and mix with the sugar and butter mixture. Ensure the egg is mixed thoroughly.

Step 3
Prepare your flour, add your baking powder, and then mix it. Add the flour to the mixture you made and mix the flour gently with a baking spatula until soft.

Step 4
Put in the oven for 40 minutes and allow it to cool before serving.

Fruit Cake

INGREDIENTS

- Butter – 1kg
- Brown Sugar – 750g
- Softener – 2 Teaspoons
- Brandy – 2 Tablespoons
- Vanilla Essence – 2 teaspoons
- Egg – 15 Large Eggs
- Flour – 1kg
- Baking Powder – 1 Tablespoon
- Mixed Fruit – 2.5 Pack
- Mixed Spice 60g
- Lemon Peel
- Cinnamon – 30g

METHOD

Step 1
Measure your brandy and use it to soak the mixed fruit and lemon peel.

Step 2
Mix your butter with the brown sugar. While mixing, add vanilla and softener with the black treacle and mix properly.

Step 3
Prepare your flour and add your mixed spice, cinnamon, and baking powder; sift all together.

Step 4
When your butter and sugar are mixed thoroughly, add your eggs and mix them. When ready, add your browning and flour. Add your mixed fruit and mix thoroughly.

Step 5
Put in the oven to bake.

Step 6
After cake is baked, inject brandy to preserve it.

Drinks

Their dreams ride the attraction of that cold, homemade drink,
navigating the sweet currents to dance in the air. They try hard to
resist the cold brew, but it's irresistible... they get
up and reach for a glass.

Tumeric Drink

INGREDIENTS

- 500mg Turmeric
- 5 or 6 Pieces of Onions
- 200g of Lemongrass
- 1kg of Ginger
- 200g Garlic
- 7 or 8 Pieces of Lemon.
- 7 Tablespoons of Honey

METHOD 1

Step 1
Peel turmeric, onions, ginger, and garlic – cut them into small sizes. Wash well and blend until smooth.

Step 2
Wash the lemongrass and put it in a pot; add 3 liters of water and boil.

Step 3
Add 7 or 8 pieces of lemon, remove the seed, and include 7 tablespoons of honey.

Step 4
Cook it for 15 minutes. When cool, put it in the refrigerator.

–Drink 100mls daily before breakfast.

METHOD 2

INGREDIENTS

- 8 Lemongrass
- 2 Big Onions
- 1 Clove of Garlic
- 2 Teaspoons of Turmeric
- 6 Teaspoons of Ginger
- Juice of 1 Lemon
- 2 Teaspoons of Honey

Follow the instructions in Method 1.

Cold Brew Iced Raspberry Tea

Kemi

This recipe makes up to a gallon of cold brew iced tea.

INGREDIENTS (Serves 16)

- 16 Cups of Distilled Water
- 8–10 Raspberry Teabags
- 1.5 Cups of Ice
- 1 Cup of Distilled Water
- 1 Cup of Sugar
- Optional: Fresh or Frozen Raspberries

METHOD

Step 1
Place 8–10 raspberry teabags in a jug and fill it with 16 cups of water.

Step 2
Add 1.5 cups of ice and place in the fridge to steep for 24 hours with a closed lid or covering.

Step 3
Squeeze and remove teabags from jug once the tea is fully steeped, leaving the cold-brewed herbal tea in the jug.

To Make Simple Syrup:

Step 4
Pour 1 cup of distilled water and 1 cup of sugar into a saucepan and put the saucepan on the stove at medium temperature. Stir the water and sugar until the sugar is completely dissolved, leaving the saucepan on until the water and sugar have boiled.

Step 5
Immediately remove the saucepan and let the simple syrup cool before pouring it into an airtight container for storage.

Simple syrup, if refrigerated, should last for 4-6 months.

To Serve:
Pour cold brew herbal tea into a glass. Add simple syrup and fresh or frozen raspberries, as you prefer. Enjoy!

Snacks

The varied snacks blossomed in the kitchen with their own special fragrance. The toasty colors of the snacks speak to their freshness and the bold flavours to come.

Puff Puff

INGREDIENTS (Serves 2)

- 2 Cups of Groundnut Oil
- 4 Cups of Flour
- 20 Cubes of Sugar
- 2.5 Cups of Palm Wine

METHOD

Step 1
From the previous evening:
Sift flour into a bowl.
Add 14 cubes of sugar to the palm wine.

Step 2
Create a hole in the flour and add the palm wine in small quantities. Mix until it is smooth. Cover mixture and leave until morning.

Step 3
Next day:
Pour groundnut oil into a frying pan. When hot, fry small balls of the mixture.

Step 4
When the balls are brown, remove them from the hot oil. When cooled, sprinkle with sugar. They can be served either hot or cold.

Chin Chin

INGREDIENTS (Serves 4)

- 4 Cups of Flour
- 2 Tablespoons of Sugar
- 4 Eggs
- 1 Cup of Water

METHOD

Step 1
Beat the eggs and mix them in a bowl

Step 2
Mix the sugar with the water to form sugar liquid, add the sugar liquid to the eggs and mix with the flour. Mix all together to form a dough.

Step 3
Knead the dough on a flat wooden board until very smooth. Use a round wooden rolling pin to flatten the mixture.

Step 4
Cut into small pieces and fry in hot oil until brown. Remove from the pan and drain out the oil.

Step 5
Store in an airtight container to retain the crunch.

Banana Fritters

INGREDIENTS (Serves 2)

- 4 Ripe Bananas
- 2 Eggs
- ¾ Cups of Flour
- 1 Cup of Water
- Sugar

METHOD

Step 1
Mash the banana until very smooth.

Step 2
Separate the yoke of the egg from the white. Beat the egg white to use as a batter.
Add the egg yolk, flour, and sugar to the mashed banana. Beat well and wrap in the beaten egg white.

Step 3
Fry in the desired size in shallow oil over a low fire.

Serve hot.

Trifle

INGREDIENTS (Serves 2)

- Soft Baked Sponge Cake
- Cooked Custard
- Jelly
- Sliced Cooked Apple

METHOD

Step 1
Crumble sponge cake on the first layer of a hollow dish.
Pour in already-made custard

Step 2
Lay in the sliced cooked apple and then pour in the jelly.

Step 3
Cover with foil paper and leave in the fridge overnight.

Family Specialties
With Great Grandma

Family – that's what we are, that is us, that is for life,
that is our forever, that is our promise, wrapped up
lovingly with great tasting food from all of us...

Sade's Recipes

Recipes in themselves have no souls; thus, the Cook must bring the soul to the recipe, and what better place to start than the versatile Stew recipe, as it forms the basis for most of the other dishes. It is a staple for most dishes listed here, making it such a good starting point.

Stew (*Obe*)

INGREDIENTS AND MEASUREMENTS
(Serves 6)

- 3Ibs Beef or Chicken
- 1 Can of Tomato
- 2 Medium Onions
- 2-3 Cloves of Garlic
- ½ Teaspoon of Salt to boil the meat (*another level tablespoon of salt to add to the rice*)
- 1 Large Red Bell Pepper (*ata nla*)
- 3-4 Habanero Peppers (*ata rodo*)
- 6-8 Thai Peppers (*ata wewe*)
- 1-2 Knorr Bouillon Cubes
- My Spice Mix (combination above)
- 1 ½ Cups of Vegetable oil (*can substitute any other desired oil*)

METHOD

Cut meat into desired size, wash thoroughly and place in a deep pot.

Add 1 chopped onion, crushed garlic, Sade's spice mix (see combination above) and let boil for about 15–20 minutes. *I tend to boil my meats for a shorter time, as I still grill them, which means they are still cooking on the grill.* Add the cooked meat to the stew and allow it to cook some more. There is no fear of it being undercooked, as it will go through at least three cooking stages. However, there is a fear of it being overcooked, which means it comes out too soft, and easily breaks or disintegrates in the stew. Use a slotted spoon to remove it from the pot and place it on an aluminum-lined metal tray.

Place in the oven, and broil or grill for about 15–20 minutes or until desired brownness is achieved.

Blend peppers (*see above for the proportions; adjust proportions as desired. For instance, if you prefer a milder taste, add more tomato, and if a more spicy and hotter taste is desired, add more of each or any of the peppers*). Then add the broth from the boiled meat to the tomato and pepper blend, blending over and over until it is a nice, smooth, lighter red consistency.

Pour oil into a pot to heat up. When hot enough, add the blended pepper mix, and cover for about 10 minutes, then lower the heat to medium-low. Let cook for another 10-15 minutes, then turn the heat to very low.

Add grilled meat to the cooking sauce, and place the lid on for another 5-8 minutes, still on extremely low heat. That allows the meats to absorb some of the stew while continuing to soften.

Stew is cooked and ready to add to your dish.

Ata Din Din (Fried Stew)

I added this as a quick bonus following the stew, as ata din din is really stew that is cooked for a bit longer that gets dried up and fried from the process. One quick tip is that you don't want to turn a full pot of stew into *ata din din*. It usually works with smaller portions. I tend to turn my left-over stew (*stew that has had all its meat eaten, but there is still excess stew left over in the pot*). Now, there is absolutely nothing wrong with this left-over stew, and it can always be put to very good use. That is the perfect base for *ata din din*.

INGREDIENTS AND MEASUREMENTS
(Serves 2)

• Leftover stew
• Ground Dry Crayfish (or Dried Shrimps)

METHOD

The stew is already cooked and leftover in a pot, so you turn the heat on at very low temperature. Add about ¼ cup of oil and place the lid on the pot. Leave to cook for 10 minutes. Keep checking until desired consistency is achieved. The stew tends to get thicker and darker. If it is too thick (*as some people like a more fluid consistency*), add a bit more oil.

This is nice with bread, yam, fried plantains (*dodo*), gizzdodo, stewed beans, boiled beans (*ewa Aganyin*). *Ewa Aganyin* is beans cooked to very soft, almost watery consistency.

Aganyins are a West African tribe, so perhaps this method of cooking beans originated from them.

Jollof Rice

Jollof rice is probably the most common African dish, and different African countries seem to have a food fight as to which country cooks the best Jollof rice. Whichever country it is, the effect of jollof rice is rice that has absorbed the stew; it is cooked in stew to turn it from white rice to colored rice. It will be an interesting project to find out how the name "Jollof" came about. Hmmm... perhaps it originated from the *Wolof (Jollof) people of West Africa. Perhaps. Let's just say that every country enjoys its own jollof rice!

The above stew recipe is the base recipe for the jollof rice.

INGREDIENTS AND MEASUREMENTS
(Serves 8)

• 3Ibs Beef or Chicken
• 1 Can of Tomato
• 2 Medium Onions
• 2-3 Cloves of Garlic
• ½ Teaspoon of Salt to Boil the Meat (*another level tablespoon of salt added to the rice*)
• 1 Large Red Bell Pepper (*ata nla*)
• 3–4 Habanero Peppers (*ata rodo*)
• 6–8 Thai Peppers (*ata wewe*)
• 1–2 Knorr Bouillon Cubes
• My Spice Mix (*combination above*)
• 4–5 Cups of Rice
• 1 Cup of Vegetable Oil (*can be substituted with Canola Oil or any other oils of your choice*).
• 2 Tablespoons of Margarine or Butter
• 1 Teaspoon of Thyme
• Water (*a quart to start with, and then added through the cooking process for desired consistency of the rice*).

METHOD

Clean meat and add to the cooking pot. Ensure your cooking pot is deep to allow the rice room to cook and spread.

Cut or chop in the onions, crush the garlic, and add that to the meat. Add all of "Sade's recommended spices" as above to the meat, including the bouillon cubes and a little water to bring the meat to boil. Cover with a lid and let cook for about 20 minutes. Set aside for about 5 minutes to cool. Take out the meat, place it on a metal tray lined with aluminum foil, and place in the oven to broil (grill). There should be broth left in the pot.

While the meat is boiling, place the rice in a deep bowl, and wash out as much of the starch as possible. Leaving the starch in the rice is what sometimes causes the jollof rice to stick together and be mushy. After it has been washed properly, drain all the water out, and set it aside.

Blend all the peppers and onion in a blender, add the broth, and blend until a smooth consistency is achieved.

You can wash the same pot used to boil the meat or use a different pot. As stated before, ensure that the pot is deep. Pour in the 1 cup of oil, add the pepper mix, cover, and leave to cook on medium heat for about 20 minutes. If it begins to bubble, lower the heat, and lilt the cover to let out some of the steam.

When you determine that the stew has cooked (*don't worry about whether it has cooked completely, as the stew continues to cook even after the rice has been poured into it. Just let it cook some*), then scoop the washed rice into the stew. Ensure that you have lowered the heat on the stew, as leaving it on medium or high will cause it to splatter and can splatter on you. Be careful as you put the rice in the stew. When you have put in all the rice, scoop in the margarine, add the thyme, add the salt, add about a cup of water, and then cover the pot to let it simmer. At this point, the heat must absolutely be on low, as this is what determines how well the jollof rice turns out. Leave covered for about 5-10 minutes, checking intermittently to see if there is still water. It is the steam from the water that cooks the rice. It is always best to have a cup of water to the side (*usually, I pour water in the blender to rinse out the blended pepper. I then pour that water into the pot of rice as it cooks*).

In pouring the water in, use a spoon to create small gaps in the rice; it is in these gaps that you pour the water into. Each time you pour water in, cover immediately, and let cook for another 5-10 minutes. You will go through these cycles as many times as necessary, and while on about the third or fourth cycle scoop a tiny bit of the cooking jollof rice onto a teaspoon to check for desired softness. The longest wait period in this whole process of cooking the jollof rice is after the rice has been put into the stew and you start checking to get the desired softness or firmness.

One tip to ensuring that your jollof rice is not mushy is, when turning it over, each time you add water, DO NOT stir. Scoop up the rice, and turn it over at different points, scooping the bottom part up and allowing the top section to go to the bottom. The reason is that the rice is cooking from the bottom up, and to get the entire pot to cook evenly, you must rotate the sections. So, the right order is "bottom up, top down" – do that each time you add water. Turn it over first, and then add the water. This process takes time, patience, and repetition until you get your desired result.

Your jollof rice is ready to eat!

One Quick Tip:

Getting an almost fresh taste to your jollof rice the following day requires that you add a bit of water, place it on very low heat, and almost cook it again for another 10-15 minutes. It will come out looking and tasting like you just cooked it. *The microwave works to warm the rice, but it does not get the same results as it was freshly cooked.

Oh, by the way, while waiting for the rice to get cooked, I took a quick reference trip to the internet and came up with this fact: Jollof is believed to have originated in the Senegambia region of West Africa among the Wolof people.

Stewed Beans (*Ewa Riro, Aka Ewa 'Beji* – Beans For Twins)

It is probably called "beans for twins" because of its high nutritional value. Folklore had it that when women of childbearing age eat ewa riro, there was a high probability that they would have twin babies. Whether this was true or not, I do not know. However, *ewa riro* is a delicious mode of cooking beans, which has high protein value, in contrast to carbohydrates, and is light enough to eat as a meal without feeling too 'heavy' from eating it.

Ewa goes well with any meat, but it is preferable to eat it with fish stew.

INGREDIENTS AND MEASUREMENTS
(Serves 8)

• 3 Cups of Black-Eyed Beans or Honey Beans (*ewa oloyin*) or Red Beans (*ewa pupa*).
• 2 Onions
• 1 Red Bell Pepper
• 2–3 Habanero Peppers
• 4–6 Thai Peppers
• 2–3 Tomatoes
• 2 Knorr Bouillon Cubes
• ½ Teaspoon of Salt
• 2 Full Tablespoons of Ground, Dry Crayfish or Shrimps
• 1 Cup of Sweet Corn
• 1/3 Cup of Palm Oil (*vegetable or any other oil could be used to substitute*)
• 1 Gallon of water

METHOD

Pick out stones and chaff from beans. This is very important, as biting into stones or chaff while eating beans or rice dish can be a big put-off from ever wanting to eat these in the future.

Rinse out the beans thoroughly and place in a deep-seated pot. Add the water. Chop 1 onion into it, add the salt and cover it. Allow to cook on medium heat for 30-45 minutes.

Beans tend to take time to cook, so check to see if they are beginning to soften. (*A pressure cooker can also be used to cook the beans, as this allows them to cook a bit faster. This is a personal preference*).

If the water is drying up, add another quart of water and turn the heat down to low or medium. Keep checking by using a teaspoon to check for softness. Beans taste better when soft, and almost pureed. You may keep adding water until you get your desired consistency.

While waiting for the beans to cook, add all pepper and onion into the blender. Also blend the bouillon cubes and crayfish or shrimps with the pepper and set aside.

When the desired consistency of beans is attained, pour in the pepper mix, and cover. Now, keep it on low or medium heat, to allow the pepper mix to cook into the beans, for 10 minutes.

Remove the pot lid, pour in the oil and sweet corn, place lid back on and reduce the heat to low. Let cook for 20-25 minutes on very low heat.

Beans should be ready to eat.

Beans can be eaten by itself, with the *ata din din* (*see above*), and a sprinkle of fine garri, or as a side with dodo (fried plantain), with rice, or with bread.

Gizzdodo

This is a relatively new combo for a side dish. It combines chicken gizzards with *dodo* (ripe plantain). Of course, you can imagine that this is always a popular option for *dodo* "lovers". It can work as a full meal but is usually served as a side to complement a main dish. As the name implies, the two main ingredients are chicken gizzards and fried plantain (*dodo*). However, a critical component of the dish is fried stew to bind the gizzards and the *dodo* together and make it more flavorful.

INGREDIENTS AND MEASUREMENTS
(Serves 8)

- 2Ibs of Chicken Gizzard (*can substitute turkey gizzards; chicken gizzards are more available*)
- 1 Medium Onion
- 2 Cloves of Garlic
- Sade's Standard Spice Mix (see above)
- 1 Tablespoon of Olive Oil
- Cooked Stew
- 6–8 Ripe but moderately firm Plantains

METHOD

Step 1

Cut the bigger-sized gizzards into smaller bite-sized pieces. Wash thoroughly, and trim off fat or unwanted parts. Rinse over, and place in a colander to drain off excess water. Set aside for about 5-10 minutes as excess water drains.

Step 2

Place gizzards in a pot, add the chopped onions, crushed garlic, combination spices as above, and tablespoon of olive oil and boil for about 10-15 minutes. Use a slotted spoon to take out the gizzards, place them on aluminum foil in a metal tray and place in the oven to broil or grill on low heat.

Step 3

If you have already made stew, you can scoop out about 3–4 cooking spoons into a pot. Place on low heat, and allow to cook for about 10 minutes, until it almost begins drying out. By now, gizzards in the oven should be nicely brown and crisp. Ensure that you take it out of

the oven before it gets too dry – it should still have a slight moistness. Add the gizzards to the "dried" stew and stir, leaving on very low heat, as the stew gets absorbed into the gizzards. Keep on low heat for another 5–10 minutes.

Step 4

Cut up (dice) the plantains, and sprinkle salt over it. Shake over to ensure salt gets on evenly. Fry in deep oil until desired brownness is achieved. Scoop out of oil and place them on paper towels to absorb excess oil. Then turn over fried plantains into the gizzard stew combo and stir. Take off the heat and set aside. Do not cover, as you do not want the fried plantain part of the gizzdodo to get soggy from covering the pot.

Gizzdodo can be eaten as a light meal with *ata din din* or as a side to other dishes like rice. If you prefer to have your gizzdodo saucier, then have more stew to start with, and increase or decrease the proportions of gizzards and the *dodo* to how much of it you want in the sauce. I tend to prefer less sauce, as the function of the sauce is to serve as a base for binding the gizzards with the dodo, so you do not want more sauce than the quantity of gizzard and dodo.

Moin-Moin

Moin-moin is simply a steamed pureed bean mixture. It's just another delicious way to enjoy your beans. Moin-moin is one of the most popular dinner menus, especially on party dinner menus, and the naira to dollar cost of making moin-moin is usually one of the higher costs on any dinner menu list. This is because moin-moin is very laborious, and everyone loves it, especially if it is well made. You almost get the feeling that it melts into your mouth, hence the name moin-moin (*Yoruba – meaning that it tends to melt into the mouth*).

Some have referred to it as moin-moin *elemi meje* (*moin-moin that has seven "lives or souls" – just a "folklore" way of saying it has seven or more ingredients; however, many ingredients were used to make it*). It is said that the more ingredients you use in making it, the tastier it is. However, keep in mind that too much of something or everything can also be bad. Let us see if my moin-moin will have *emi meje,* or perhaps more... :))

INGREDIENTS AND MEASUREMENTS
(Serves 8)

_____

• 3 Cups of Red Beans (*ewa pupa*), Honey Beans (*ewa oloyin*) or Black-Eyed Beans
• 1 Large Onion
• 2 Large Red Bell Peppers
• 3-4 Habanero Peppers
• 6-8 Thai Peppers
• 2-3 Tomatoes
• 3 Knorr Bouillon Cubes
• 1 Teaspoon of Salt
• 3 Full Tablespoons of Ground, Dry Crayfish or Shrimps
• 1 Cup of Chopped Liver
• 1 Cup of Chopped Fish Bits
• 1 Tin of Corned Beef
• 6 Eggs
• 1 Cup of Olive Oil (*can use desirable substitute*)
• 2 Garlic Cloves
• Meat Broth
• 8 Mini Bread Pans (or 12 small milk cans; or native wrap leaves – *ewe*)

• A Big, Deep (*deep enough to layer it up*) Pot for cooking the Moin-Moin

METHOD

Pick out the chaff from beans. Soak beans in water for about 30 minutes to one hour. Peel skin off beans. Various methods exist for doing that. My preferred method is to scoop beans on a rough surface, native grinding small table size, or a wide brim mortar, using the pestle. Gently grind beans in small portions against a rough surface until the skin peels off the beans – do that for the entire batch.

Then, in a big, wide bowl, run water through the beans, sieving them to separate the skin from the beans. This is very time consuming and laborious, but I do it until I get every bit of skin off the beans. Place 5 eggs in a pot and bring to boil. Set it aside.

Rinse out the beans a few more times and drain off the water. Have another big, wide bowl set aside.

Cut up all the peppers, onion, and tomatoes into the beans. Using a ladle, scoop a handful of the peeled beans with a bit of water into a blender, and blend. You are going to blend a couple of rounds, so there is no need for the beans to be completely smooth this first time around. Repeat the cycle until all the beans have gone through the first round of blending. Rinse out the first bowl, and reverse the process, blending again the full bowl of beans, about two-ladle full at a time. Add a bit of water if it is too thick or if you notice the blender is having difficulty blending. You do not want to put too much in the blender at a time so as not to strain the blender motor. You will notice that it blends easily once you add a bit of water. However, do not add too much water, as you do not want to dilute your mixture.

When blending the second time around, add the Knorr cubes, the crayfish, shrimps, and meat broth, and blend with the mixture. By the end of the second-round blend, your mixture should have a very smooth consistency. If it is not smooth enough, repeat the blending process. By this time, you should have a slightly red, very smooth mixture.

Now you're ready to complete the mixture for the moin-moin. Crush the garlic into a bowl and pour the oil into it. Microwave the garlic and oil to allow the garlic to be infused into the oil. Pour about ¾ of the blend into the ground beans mixture. Stir continuously for about 5 minutes. Add the other ingredients: copped cooked liver, chopped cooked fish pieces, corned beef, and salt. Stir again with a bit of power, as you want all the ingredients to combine well together.

Taste for salt. Moin-moin always requires more than the average amount of salt to get the appropriate salt taste. If necessary, add a bit more salt.

Break one egg into the mix and stir hard again for about 5 minutes.

Open the corned beef tin and stir into the mixture. Loosen any chunks or lumps of corned beef, so it spreads evenly in the mixture. Stir for 3-5 minutes. Set aside.

Crack open the boiled eggs, cut up into halves, and set these aside.

Using a kitchen brush, brush the oil and garlic blend lavishly all around the inside of the mini foil pans. Then, using the ladle,

scoop 2–3 ladle-spoon full into each mini pan (*or native leaf wrap – you must know how to fold these correctly; otherwise, the moin-moin mix will slip out of the leaves, and create a mess while cooking*).

Put each half of the boiled egg into each mini-pan of moin-moin mix. Cut up aluminum foil into square sizes to cover each mini aluminum-foil pan.

Pour water up to half the cooking pot, and gently place the mini pans (*or folded moin-moin leaves*) neatly, methodically, and evenly in the pot, then cover it.

Turn the heat to high for 5-8 minutes to allow the water in the pot to heat up. Then lower the heat to low to allow the steam from the water to cook the moin-moin. You may need to add water to the bottom of the pot a few times as it evaporates to allow the moin-moin cook evenly and well.

The cooking time could be up to one hour. When the moin-moin is cooked, it will have a soft consistency. Some people like it that

soft and are ready to eat it as soon as it gets off the stove. Some people prefer it to be a bit firmer. It is always going to get firm. If you prefer it firm, take it out of the pot, turn it over onto your plate, and set it aside for about 5–10 minutes, it will firm up.

Leftover moin-moin is best enjoyed reheated instead of warming in the microwave.

I am sure we can count seven and perhaps more *"emis"* in this moin-moin. After all the hard work, please enjoy!!!

Sea Food Pepper Soup or Sea Food Gumbo

Seafood!!! Seafood is my preferred form of meat, and though I do not fancy every seafood, I like quite a few. I beg to skip on the octopus, squids, oysters, etc. However, give me the fish, crabs, and shrimps, and we are good to go. Pepper soup is a health remedy dish for days when one is sick or lethargic, and seafood is a nice, easy, soft healthy meat, which together can make a delicious, light meal to substitute a heavy meal for those kinds of days – light, healthy meal days! Gumbo simply means a combination of different food items.

INGREDIENTS AND MEASUREMENTS
(Serves 4)

• Assorted Seafood of your liking (Fish, Crab-meat, Shrimps, Fresh Crayfish)
• 2 Cloves of Garlic (*or Tablespoon of my garlic and olive oil infused mix referenced above*)
• 2 Teaspoons of Ginger (*grated, pureed, or powder*)
• ½ Teaspoon Ground White Pepper
• ½ Teaspoon Ground Black Pepper
• 1 tablespoon Ground Red Hot Pepper
• ½ Teaspoon Ground Cameroonian Hot Pepper
• 1 Fish Bouillon or 2 Beef Knorr Cubes
• 2–3 Tablespoons of Pepper Soup Mix (*this item is available in the markets or stores but is primarily made up of different local spices. If you can't find this, you can substitute with a bit more of the above. Just double it up to give a more flavored taste*).
• A Pinch of Ground Dry Bitter Leaves, to give a slightly bitter taste (*This is optional and depends on your desired taste*).
• 1 Quart of Water
• 3 Tablespoons of Olive Oil
• ½ Teaspoon of Salt

METHOD

Step 1
Clean and rinse out all your desired fresh

food. Ensure that it has not gone bad, as fresh seafood has the propensity to go bad quickly. If it was purchased the day before, keep it refrigerated until ready to use. Put in a strainer to strain out excess water. Set aside. After it has drained the excess water, add the garlic, turn it over a few times, and then set aside.

Step 2
Pour water into a pot, preferably a deep pot.

For this fish dish, the seafood breaking up into pieces is not much of an issue. This is a combo dish, and the idea is that all the ingredients come together in combo form.

Place pot on the stovetop and keep at medium heat.

Step 3
One option is to place all the above dry ingredients in a food processor or blender and blend together, then pour them into the water, or to add each ingredient one after the other until all have been added. Either way, put all the dry ingredients in.

Step 4
Let the water and ingredient mix cook for about 15–20 minutes. Taste to ensure it's not too salty; if it needs something more, add more of whichever ingredients you desire. For instance, if you want it hot spicy, you can choose to add a bit more of the red hot or Cameroonian pepper. Follow your preferred taste. If you want it more savory, add one more bouillon (*fish or beef*). If you do add more of the spices, allow it to simmer for another 6-7 minutes on medium heat.

Step 5
Slowly add the different seafood. Do not stir, as seafood gets soft quickly, and you don't want it too mushy. It will eventually get there if there are more leftovers remaining after a day. That first day, you still want to be able to identify the different seafood pieces.

Step 6
Reduce heat to low or medium and cover the pot for another 10-15 minutes.

Your seafood pepper soup is ready.

One Gentle Hint
Use a ladle to scoop the soup and start with scooping out the seafood first and then the liquid soup atop it. You can eat it by itself or with a dinner rolls on the side. Have a glass of cold beverage handy!

Efo Riro With Leftover Stew

Let me throw in another quick one that derives from my leftover stew referenced above. As I stated above, leftover stew never goes to waste in my kitchen. Yesterday's bottom of the pot is today's efo riro.

INGREDIENTS AND MEASUREMENTS
(Serves 5)

• Leftover Stew (*whatever amount is left over*)
• 1 Tablespoon of Ground Dry Crayfish (*or Dried Shrimps*)
• 1lb of or about 15–20 Count Raw Shrimps (*medium or large size*)
• 1 Tablespoon of Ground, Dry Bitter Leaves (*ewuro*)
• 1 Small Onion
• ¼ Cup of Oil (*any desired oil; I prefer olive oil*)
• 2 Cloves of Garlic
• 2 7–10oz Bags of Cleaned out Spinach (*or any other vegetable of choice*).

METHOD

Boil water, pour over the spinach, and then squeeze out the water. Keep squeezing until you get as much water out as possible. They will look like little rolls after the squeeze. Set aside.

Leftover stew is already in the pot because, of course, it is leftover. You can choose to scoop it out into a clean pot to set a presentable look of being made afresh or keep it in the same pot it was made. Place pot with stew on extremely low heat. Slice or chop the onion into it. Leave to cook for 5–8 minutes.

While it's cooking, clean the raw shrimps, and place them in a sieve to remove excess water. Then crush garlic into a bowl, add a tablespoon of oil to the garlic, and microwave for 30 seconds.

Pour garlic and oil blend onto the raw shrimps and turn over or toss a couple of times. Set aside.

Add dry crayfish and dry bitter leaves into the stew cooking. By now, the stew will be drying up and browning. The added dry crayfish and bitter leaves will turn it even darker.

Then add the raw shrimps and the oil, stir for a quick second, cover and leave to cook for another 5–8 minutes. Look to see that the shrimps have turned pink to indicate that they are cooked; stir a bit more to get the stew sauce well into the shrimps.

Then spread the spinach into the stew mix and stir around for a bit to get them all blended, and that is your stewed efo riro! It will have a slightly bitter, savory taste. That is the bitter leaves' flavor. If you do not like that taste or prefer less of it, then do not add bitter leaves at all or reduce the amount of it that you add.

This is a nice side dish to rice or any other main meal for that matter!

Seyi's Special Salad

INGREDIENTS

The quantities required for the listed ingredients are omitted because you can put as much or as little of each or completely leave out some as you desire. This is all a matter of personal preference and or availability.

• 7-10 oz. Bag of Butter Lettuce.
Butter lettuce is great because it has a smooth, soft taste, almost buttery, and it looks very appetizing, especially when it is fresh. If this is not available, any other variety of salad leaves will work just as well. Like I said about salads, it is really a matter of preference and what is available.

• Crumbled Blue cheese or crumbled Feta cheese

• Nuts (any desired nuts will do – walnuts, pecans, almonds, etc.)
It is preferred to have them in pieces rather than whole. Whatever variety of nuts you like will work. You can also do a combination of nuts.

• Mandarin orange sections.
This can also be substituted with any desired fruits, preferably fruits with some sweetness, such as red or green grapes, pineapple, apples).

• Dried fruits such as cranberries, raisins, or apricot.

• Chicken, meat, or fillet of fish (any preferred fish, ensure it is the fillet).
For chicken, it's best to use chicken breast, as it is the meatiest part of the chicken. It can be grilled or fried.

• Salad dressing (preferably a sweet-based one)

METHOD

Place butter lettuce in a wide salad bowl.

Add desired quantities of all listed ingredients, and it is ready to eat!

Best to approximate the right size you can eat in one sitting, as it doesn't keep well if left overnight. The salad leaves will shrivel, and the entire salad will become soggy and undesirable.

Tolu's Recipes

The joys of life are right here before us, stories of the years told in wisps of aroma and tastes that are time machines to many good memories. If flavors could get off the table and do an energetic dance, these flavors would do just that.

Meat Stew

INGREDIENTS (Serves 6)

• 4 Red Bell Peppers Chopped
• 2–3 Small Spicy Pepper Chopped
• 1 Medium Onion, Peeled and Chopped
• I Medium Can of Whole Tomatoes
• 1 Small Can of Tomato Paste
• 3–4 Pound Beef or Lamb or Goat or Stew Meat, Trimmed and Cut into Cubes
• 5 Tablespoons of Vegetable Oil
• 1 Cup Beef Broth (*homemade*)
• Beef Cubes
• Salt to taste

METHOD

Step 1

Boil cut meat in a pot and season with salt, ginger, onions, thyme, and garlic, then drain beef broth into a bowl when done.

Step 2
Combine the chopped pepper (*bell and spicy*), can of whole tomatoes, and chopped onion in a bowl, grind for a mixed ingredient.

Step 3
Heat the oil in a large pot and add the beef for 3 minutes. Cook, turning the pieces until beef is browned on all sides.

Step 4
Remove the beef from the pot and add the mixed ingredients and 5 cups of water. Cook over medium-high heat for 30 minutes, stirring occasionally.

Step 5
Add the tomato paste and cook for another 20 minutes until the ingredients are cooked.

Step 6
Add the beef, beef broth, and beef cubes. Bring to a boil, then reduce to a slow simmer. Cover and cook, skimming broth from time to time. Add broth or water if the stew is dry.

Season with salt and pepper to taste.

Grilled Whole Turkey

INGREDIENTS (Serves 6)

- Medium Size Turkey
- 1 Medium Onion, Peeled and Chopped
- 1 Tablespoon Vegetable Oil
- 2 Cups Beef Broth (*homemade*)
- 2 Beef Flavor Cubes
- Salt to taste
- 1 Tablespoon Chopped Garlic or Garlic Powder
- 2 Tablespoons Smoked Paprika
- 1 Tablespoon of Spicy Pepper Powder
- 1 Tablespoon of Barbecue Seasoning
- Lettuce
- Grape Tomato
- Sliced Onion

METHOD

Step 1
Clean out Turkey. Rinse and pat dry with kitchen paper roll.

Step 2
Mix seasoning in a small bowl, adding a drop of water – chopped garlic or garlic powder, smoked paprika, spicy pepper powder, onions, meat broth, and barbecue seasoning. Add half a teaspoon of oil. Use a kitchen brush to marinate the seasoning all over and inside the Turkey numerous times.

Step 3
Wrap the turkey completely with cling film and leave to marinate overnight.

Step 4
Next morning. Marinate again and spray oil all over. (*I also smear a bit of honey sometimes around before I spray with oil*). You can also use a brush to spread the oil.

Step 5
Put the turkey in the oven. My default temperature is 360 degrees but check as your oven will guide. Ensure heat is getting to all areas of the turkey evenly.

Step 6
When cooked (*make sure it is fully cooked right inside*), dress on a plate with stuffing, lettuce, and tomatoes or whatever you have.

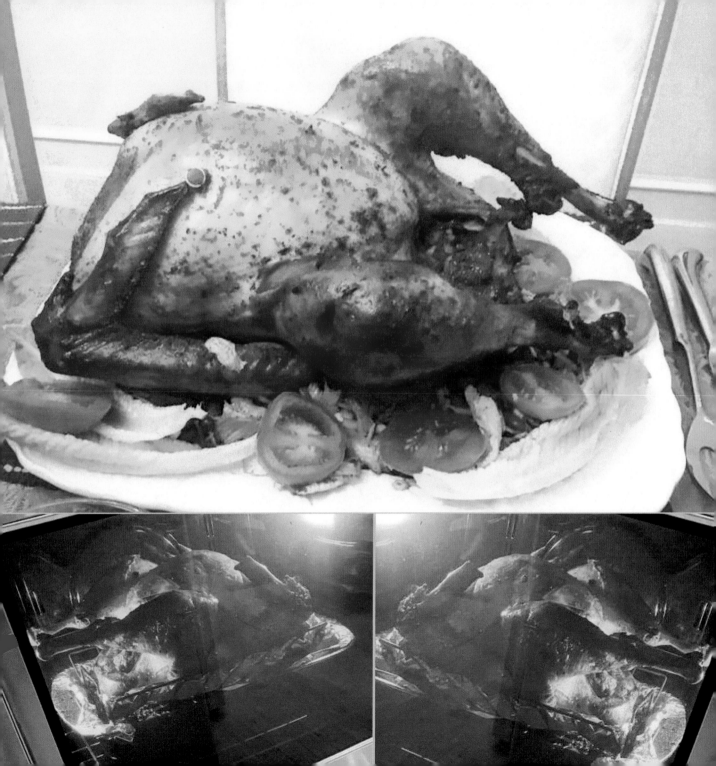

Temilade's Recipe

Flavorful cooking has a way of perfuming the air to tease one,
not as some bottled fragrances would, yet in a similar
way that flowers give their fragrance to the breeze.

Ribeye Steak With Peppercorn Sauce and Mashed Potatoes

INGREDIENTS (Serves 2)

- 2 Bone-in Ribeye Steak (200g each)
- 3 Cloves of Garlic
- Finely Chopped Parsley
- Finely Chopped Basil
- 100g of Unsalted Butter
- 2 Teaspoon of Black Peppercorn
- 3 Teaspoon of Red Wine
- 1 Teaspoon of Salt
- 1 Teaspoon of Black Pepper
- 2 Tablespoons of Yellow Pepper
- 2 Tablespoon of Chili Pepper
- ¼ Cup of Beef Broth
- 5 Medium Potatoes (diced)
- Cooking Cream or Flour

METHOD

Step 1

Heat a well-seasoned cast-iron skillet over high heat until it's smoking. Using paper towels, pat both sides of the steak until dry. Marinate the steak with salt, black pepper, garlic, chili pepper, parsley, basil and seasoning cubes 30 minutes before cooking.

Step 2

Include a tablespoon of oil in the skillet. When sizzling, include the clove of garlic or garlic paste. Let it fry. Immediately place the steak in the middle of the hot skillet. Cook for 1 minute without moving. Turn with tongs and cook the other side for 1 minute. Repeat this process twice.

Step 3

Push steak to one side of the skillet; add butter, garlic, chopped parsley and basil to the opposite side of the skillet, tilting the skillet towards the butter and cooking until butter is foaming for about 30 seconds to 1 minute. Working carefully, spoon butter over steak for 1–2 minutes, turning over once, until it reaches an internal temperature of 120°F or 49°C for medium-rare or until desired doneness.

Step 4

Rest the steak for 15 minutes before serving to ensure maximum juiciness.

Step 5

Peppercorn sauce: Heat butter and flour on the fire. When sizzling, include the beef broth and peppercorn – let this cook for five minutes.

Add cooking cream or flour mixed with water. Let this cook for five minutes.

Add the tablespoon of red wine, season with parsley, garlic, pepper, and seasoning cubes, if necessary.

Step 6

Bring a pot of salted water to a boil. Add potatoes and cook until tender but still firm for about 15 minutes; then drain.

Heat butter and milk over low heat in a small saucepan until butter is melted. Using a potato masher or electric beater, slowly blend milk mixture into potatoes until smooth and creamy. Season with salt and pepper to taste.

Serve the steak with sauce and mashed potatoes.

Seafood Pasta

INGREDIENTS (Serves 5)

- 1 Pack of Spaghetti Linguine
- Tomato Paste
- Finely Chopped Parsley
- Finely Chopped Basil
- Garlic Paste
- Unsalted Butter
- Prawns
- Calamari
- Big Chunks of Croaker Fish
- 1 Teaspoon of Honey
- Seasoning Cubes
- 2 Tablespoon of Chili Pepper

METHOD

Step 1
Put the spaghetti to a boil in hot water for 15 minutes. Ensure the spaghetti is not overcooked, as it will still cook in the tomato sauce. When cooked, run the spaghetti in cold water and drain. Set the spaghetti aside.

Step 2
Marinate the seafood with salt, seasoning cube, garlic, pepper, and Italian herbs. Oil the pan; when the oil is sizzling, add the chopped onions and garlic paste. Stir fry the seafood until slightly cooked.

Step 3
Remove the slightly cooked seafood from the pan and keep aside. Pour in the tomato paste and let this cook for 10 minutes. Season the tomato paste with salt, chilli pepper, a little honey, and Maggi or Knorr for taste.

Step 4
Pour in the cooked pasta and add a little bit of water if needed. Let this cook for 10 minutes. Then add the seafood mix and allow to cook for another 5 minutes.

Step 5
Add in a tablespoon of unsalted butter with freshly chopped basil and parsley. Allow to cook for 5 minutes.

The spaghetti is ready!

Grilled Fish

INGREDIENTS (Serves 3)

• Whole Seabass Fish
• Lemon
• Finely Chopped Parsley
• Finely Chopped Basil
• Garlic Paste
• Unsalted Butter
• Ginger
• Ketchup
• Seasoning Cubes
• 2 Tablespoon of Chili Pepper and Cameroon Pepper

METHOD

Step 1
Wash and clean the fish thoroughly. Spice the whole fish with seasoning cube, salt, Cameroon pepper, Italian herbs, garlic, ginger, ketchup, and unsalted butter.

Step 2
Marinate the spices inside the fish properly. Slice the lemon, squeeze the lemon juice on the fish and place the slices of lemon on the fish. Pour chopped parsley and basil on the fish.

Step 3
Wrap the fish in foil paper with unsalted butter and allow to marinate for an hour. Put fish in the oven at 170 degrees.

Step 4
Check intermittently and turn around until well cooked.

Step 5
Garnish with lemon, herbs, and lettuce.

The fish is ready!

Seafood Okro

INGREDIENTS (Serves 4)

- Okro
- Fresh Pepper
- Fresh Fish
- Prawns
- Garlic Paste
- Palm Oil
- Oziza Leaves (*Piper Guineense Leaf*)
- Calamari
- Seasoning Cubes
- Salt for taste
- Cameroon Pepper
- Onions
- Crayfish

METHOD

Step 1
Clean the fish, calamari, and prawns and season with pepper, salt, seasoning cubes.

Step 2
Cut the okro into medium sizes. Blend or pound the fresh pepper and set aside. Cut the Oziza (piper guineense) leaves and chop your onions.

Step 3
Add seasoned fish and calamari to a pot, and let it cook for 3 minutes. Then add the prawns, allow to continue cooking for 5 minutes, then set aside.

Step 4
Put a clean pot on the fire, add palm oil and heat it up for a few minutes, then add the chopped onions. Fry for 3 minutes, add the Okro and fry for another 5 minutes,

Step 5
Add meat stock and the stock from the fish and prawns, stir and allow to boil. Then add a spoon full of crayfish. Add the fish, prawns, and calamari to the pot; add seasoning cubes and salt for taste. Allow to cook for 5 minutes.

Okro soup is ready!

Sola's Recipe

From the kitchen of creation comes a bounty
that brings hearts into a song in one vibrant accord...
And indeed, this is one healthful, vibrant recipe.

Salmon & Spinach Delight

INGREDIENTS AND MEASUREMENTS
(Serves 2)

- 2 Boneless Salmon Fillets
- 500g of Baby Spinach Leaves
- 10 Baby Potatoes (250g)
- 2 Teaspoon of Crayfish
- 150g Ready Peeled King Shrimps
- 1 Scotch Bonnet Pepper
- 1/2 Large Onions
- 1/2 Knorr Chicken Cube
- 1 Teaspoon of White Pepper
- 1 Teaspoon of Black Pepper
- 1 Teaspoon of Salt
- 2 Tablespoon of Butter
- 2 Tablespoon of Chili Pepper Paste
- 2 Tablespoon of Sunflower Oil

METHOD

Step 1

Season the salmon fillet with black pepper, white pepper, and a sprinkle of salt. Then place flat on a baking tray with the skin facing up. Place this in the oven at a temperature of 180°C or 356°F for 30 minutes.

Step 2

Cut baby potatoes into two pieces. Spread butter and pepper paste over the pieces. Sprinkle salt over the potatoes and place in oven at the gas mark 180°C or 356°F for 30 minutes.

Step 3

Slice the onion and scotch bonnet pepper. Heat the sunflower oil in a pan over medium heat and fry the onions and pepper for 3 minutes. Add the shrimps and cook for 5 minutes more until just brown.

Step 4

Soak the Spinach in boiling water for 3 minutes, rinse with cold water and squeeze out the water. Chop the spinach as desired.

Step 5

Pour the chicken stock and crayfish into the pan, and then add the Spinach. Cook for 3–5 minutes more.

Step 6

Serve the Spinach with the Salmon and baby potatoes.

Tinuade's Recipe

Show me the food, and I will show you the story of our kitchen,
of generations of nurturing love and how we found both
joy and gratitude in the meals we make.

TinTin's Lasagna

Prep Time: 30 Minutes
Cook Time: 60 Minutes
Rest Time: 30 Minutes
Total Time: 1 Hour 30 Minutes

INGREDIENTS (Serves 6)

• 1kg Minced Meat
• 1 Onion – diced
• 2 Large Cloves of Garlic – minced or diced
• Oil
• 1 Jar Lasagna or Bolognese Tomato Red Sauce
• 1 Sachet Tomato Paste
• Liquid Stock or Broth
• 1/2 Cup Red Wine (optional)
• 1 Teaspoon of White Sugar (*to balance the acidity of the tomatoes*)
• Chopped Fresh Basil
• Chopped Fresh Parsley
• Thyme
• Ground Oregano (to taste)
• Salt (to taste)
• Maggi or Knorr Seasoning Cubes
• Black Pepper
• Scotch Bonnet or Habanero Peppers
• Ground Black Pepper
• 1 Pack Lasagna Noodles
• Cheese (*different types*) – *I like to mix mozzarella, Parmesan, and triangle cheeses.*

METHOD

Step 1
Spread a little oil in a large pot over medium heat. Add your minced meat. Break the meat up into small pieces with a spoon.

Add the chopped onion and garlic and cook until the meat is well browned and not pink anymore, stirring constantly.

Step 2
Pour in red wine to sizzle for 2 minutes until almost evaporated.

Step 3
Pour in tomato sauce and tomato paste.

Step 4
Stir in sugar, fresh basil, oregano, salt, Maggi or knorr seasoning, scotch bonnet or habanero peppers, black pepper, and chopped parsley.

Step 5

Stir well and bring to a simmer. Then cover and cook on low heat for about 10 minutes.

Step 6

Place lasagna noodles into the bottom of a pan or dish. Pour hot water directly over the noodles, making sure the noodles are completely immersed in the water. Let them soak for 15 minutes, then drain and discard the water. (Don't layer them on top of each other; this prevents them from sticking to each other). Alternatively, you can boil in a large pot until al dente (firm to the bite). *Your pasta box should have cooking instructions.*

Step 7

Combine your white lasagna sauce with black pepper and 2 tablespoons of parsley.

Step 8

Preheat oven to 190°C or 374°F Lightly grease a deep 9x13 inch pan

Now The Fun Part – Layering!

* To assemble, spread about 1/2 cup of meat sauce to the bottom of the prepared pan.

* Place 3 or 4 noodles on top, depending on the size of your lasagna noodles.

* Spread on 1/3 of your entire meat sauce.

* Sprinkle with a cup of cheese (*or your preferred quantity*)

* Spread the top with 1/2 of the white lasagna sauce mixture.

* Repeat until you have three layers of noodles. That means Layer noodles, 1/3 meat sauce, 1cup cheese, the 2nd 1/2 cheese sauce. Then layer the final noodles, the remaining 1/3 meat sauce, and the remaining cheese.

* Cover loosely with aluminum foil.

* Bake in preheated oven for 45 minutes.

*Remove foil and bake for an additional 15 minutes to allow the cheese to turn golden.

* Let it cool for 30 minutes, and then serve.

Cooking Tips

– By Sade

• I avoid using too many bouillon cubes of any type in all my cooking, usually one, two at the most, regardless of what I am cooking. Of course, you would use more if you were doing a large volume of cooking. I say one to two for a regular sized pot of food would be just fine. I prefer the Knorr variety.

• I grill or broil all my meats (also chicken) and fish in the oven, and they come out looking and tasting fried.

• It is desirable to cut meats into manageable sizes, particularly meats that are served for entertaining, as you do not want to put your guests in situations where the meat is either too big for them to 'tackle' within a public place or have them embarrassed from trying to figure a way to manage or eat the meats. Always err on the side of small or medium sizes. You can always heap more portions of that on the helping. Plus, it has a more appealing or desirable presentation when it is cut and served in that manner.

• I use a wide-brim, shallow cooking pot for cooking my fish stew or fish dish. This is specific to fish dishes, as it allows the fish to stay whole and intact.

• For savory dishes, regardless of what I am cooking, I sprinkle dry red-hot pepper to flavor it. I will usually combine that with Cameroonian dry-hot pepper, another variety of hot pepper. This flavors the food nicely.

• No leftovers go to waste. If I get to the bottom dredges of a pot of soup or stew, that leftover usually becomes the base for my *efo riro* (stir efo).

• Other uses for any leftover stew include transforming it to ata din din. *Ata din din* is simply fried stew eaten with bread, yam, dodo, beans (*ewa riro*), and just about anything that requires fried spicy stew to compliment it. More about preparing *ata din din* can be seen in previous pages.

• I do not over-boil or over-cook my meats, as these tend to continue to soften when added to the soup or stew.

• My standard seasonings are salt, ground ginger, ground white pepper, ground black pepper, season-all (*Old Bay variety*), ground dry red-hot pepper; ground dry hot Cameroonian pepper; Knorr cube(s), garlic cloves (*1–2 big cloves, or 2–3 medium cloves*). While I don't have a standard measurement that I use, approximately half to one full teaspoon of each will do, except for the salt, which is about a quarter or less teaspoon.

• This mix of seasoning is what I would use to season my meats (beef or chicken), and the broth from this is what I use for cooking the stew or soup. I never add new seasoning directly to the soup. Whatever taste results from the soup has been predetermined by how tasty or not tasty the broth from the meats is.

• My standard pepper or spice mix is usually made up of 1 large or 2 medium red bell pepper(s) (*tatase*), 1 large or 2 small onion(s), 3 or 4 habanero peppers (*ata rodo*) (*my soups tend to be hot spicy, so determine your level of comfort for hotness*), 6-8 Thai peppers (*ata wewe*) and 1 large can of tomato (*whole tomatoes or sauce*). Blend these with the broth from the meats that you have just cooked. I ALWAYS blend my pepper mix with the broth; it allows the broth to mix thoroughly, and smoothly to give a smooth, consistent soup.

– Caveat!! I tend to make most of my dishes quite hot and spicy, so if you do not like hot and spicy, reduce the peppers significantly, and work your way up gradually until you get your desired level.

• GARLIC! Garlic has much nutritional value, though it has an extraordinarily strong, overpowering smell. While I may not add it directly to salads, or eat it straight, I prefer to use fresh garlic cloves in all my cooking. Garlic gives the cooking a delicious taste and has numerous proven health benefits. The strong odor is neutralized or reduced by the cooking.

• To expedite my cooking, I would sometimes crush about 6–8 cloves of garlic into about half a cup of olive oil and microwave it for about 40 seconds. That serves two purposes: One, it allows the garlic to infuse into the oil, and two, it is ready to use for cooking. Then I scoop about a tablespoon of the olive oil and garlic combo into my meats or other cooking that requires garlic. The garlic gets absorbed into the food quicker when done this way.

• You may have to cook a particular dish several times, making different adjustments to portions of ingredients, before you achieve your preferred taste or consistency.

• One of my most valued cooking tips, which has served me well for all my cooking is, never to cook hurriedly (recognition to my mom, Mommy Latunji for this tip). While you may put it on high to medium heat to get it started, you MUST reduce the heat shortly after, and allow it to cook well on as little direct heat as possible. Most foods come out thoroughly and nicely cooked when cooked on extremely low heat. Also, cooking on low heat prevents the food from burning, which had happened to me on occasions when I either forgot or neglected to turn the fire or heat down.

• Always ensure that you have a lid over the cooking pot, with it slightly tilted to prevent spillover. It is the steam from the food that cooks it.

• My tips on cooking will not be complete without reference to my favorite food, fried plantains, also known as dodo! My tip on plantains is the types of cuts. You can slice, dice, or cube the plantain. Slicing it long and thinly is appropriate when the plantain is still hard or firm. The dodo comes out long and crisp – perfect for snacking. The diced cut works with soft to medium soft plantains. This is delicious with rice and beans and complements other dishes on a dinner menu. The cube cut is also like diced cut, but bigger in size. Both diced and cube cut work well in a gizzard and dodo (gizzdodo) combination dish.

• Now, this tip is perhaps the most valuable of all my tips: Always clean up as you go along. As soon as you get done with any utensil, regardless of how small it is, simply wash it, and put it away. Cooking involves multi-tasking – prepping the food, cooking it, cleaning up, and enjoying the end product. Each aspect of the task allows you to enjoy the end product. For instance, good prepping results in good cooking, good cooking results in tasty food, cleaning as you go along avoids dealing with the mess when the cooking is done, and not having to deal with the mess allows you to sit down, relax, and enjoy your nicely cooked food.

• I do not shy away from trying out new recipes or new ways of doing what I already know how to do. There's always room for learning new ways of doing things or improving on what I already know.

• Finally, how your food turns out will be based on the effort you put into making it. Cooking requires meticulous effort, passion, and love. If you are too tired to cook on a particular day or in a hurry, then do not cook on that day. That is the day you rustle up leftovers and leave the cooking for when you are ready and able to put in a good effort. That may be the day to pick up pizza or Chinese food.

There is also the possibility that you actually have enough energy to cook the food but are too tired to eat it. That is also okay. At times like that, you can enjoy the food by watching others enjoy it. That is part of the joy of cooking – enjoying having others enjoy your food. That works too!!!

Made in the USA
Middletown, DE
15 March 2023

26727428R00058